SHIPS
OF THE AIR

LYNN CURLEE

HOUGHTON MIFFLIN COMPANY   BOSTON   1996

· · BIBLIOGRAPHY · ·

COLLIER, BASIL. *The Airship: A History*. New York: G. P. Putnam's Sons, 1974.
EGE, LENNART. *Balloons and Airships*. New York: Macmillan, 1974.
HORTON, EDWARD. *The Age of the Airship*. Chicago: Henry Regnery, 1973.
JACKSON, ROBERT. *Airships*. Garden City, N.Y.: Doubleday, 1973.
NORGAARD, ERIK. *The Book of Balloons*. New York: Crown, 1971.
PAYNE, LEE. *Lighter than Air: An Illustrated History of the Airship*. New York: Orion Books, 1977.

· · · · ·

TITLE-PAGE ILLUSTRATION: *The* R-100 *at the mooring mast*

DEDICATION-PAGE ILLUSTRATION: *A French dirigible in 1906*

· · · · ·

For information about this and other Houghton Mifflin
trade and reference books and multimedia products, visit
The Bookstore at Houghton Mifflin on the World Wide Web
at http://www.hmco.com/trade/.

Manufactured in the United States of America

Book design by David Saylor
The text of this book is set in 14-point Simoncini Garamond.
The illustrations are acrylic paintings, reproduced in full color.

HOR   10   9   8   7   6   5   4   3   2   1

LIBRARY OF CONGRESS CATALOGING-IN-PUBLICATION DATA
Curlee, Lynn.   Ships of the air / Lynn Curlee.   p.   cm.   ISBN 0-395-69338-1
1. Airships—History—Juvenile Literature. 2. Balloons—History—Juvenile literature.
[1. Airships—History. 2. Balloons—History.] I. Title.
TL650.C87 1996   629.133'2—dc20   94-10746   CIP   AC

In memory of John D. Martin

PEOPLE HAVE ALWAYS dreamed of flying. For thousands of years, flying horses, chariots, and carpets have appeared in myths and legends in many parts of the world. One Greek myth tells of a boy named Icarus whose father made him wings of feathers and wax. When Icarus flew too near the sun, the wax melted and he fell into the sea. Over the centuries, inventors have suggested many ideas for flying machines. Some of the inventors also imagined ways that people might fly with wings. But it was not until 1783—more than 100 years before the first airplane—that the dream of flight finally came true.

Joseph and Étienne Montgolfier were the Frenchmen who built the first hot-air balloon. The Montgolfier brothers owned a paper-

The Montgolfier brothers launch their hot-air balloon at Versailles.

making factory. Like most educated people in the 1700s, they knew about the many scientific discoveries then taking place. And, like others of their time, they were fascinated with flight.

One day, after watching ashes from a fire float upward, Joseph Montgolfier folded a piece of paper, held it above a fire, then watched it fly up the chimney. Joseph believed that the smoky fire created some kind of gas that was lighter than air. Only later did he and Étienne understand that hot air rises. But Joseph did understand that if a big enough bag could be filled with that hot "gas," the bag would rise off the ground—and could carry a person with it.

The Montgolfier brothers experimented with cloth bags until they were ready to show other people what they had discovered. For their public demonstration, they built a 33-foot-wide balloon. It was made of silk, lined with paper, and held together with buttons in buttonholes. On June 5, 1783, hundreds of people in the brothers' hometown of Annonay, France, watched as the balloon rose about 6,000 feet. The balloon stayed aloft for only 10 minutes. It carried no passengers or source of heat, and as the air inside it cooled, the balloon gently landed.

Excited by news of the Montgolfiers' success, the French Academy of Science invited them to come to Paris. On September 19 the Montgolfiers launched a new and larger balloon from the Palace of Versailles, outside Paris. While King Louis XVI, Queen Marie

Antoinette, and the entire French court watched, the brothers lit a fire under the opening of the beautifully painted balloon. It rose into the sky carrying a basket containing the first passengers ever to ride in a balloon: a sheep, a rooster, and a duck. When the balloon returned to the ground from a height of about 1,500 feet, the animals were safe and an important discovery had been made. Until that time, some scientists had believed that the layer of air surrounding the earth was only a few hundred feet deep. Now they knew that it was much deeper and that passengers carried by a balloon would be able to breathe.

At the same time that the French Academy of Science invited the Montgolfiers to Paris, it asked Jacques Alexandre César Charles to build his own balloon. Professor Charles filled his balloon with hydrogen gas, which had been discovered in 1766. Hydrogen is much lighter than air, so it rises without having to be heated. Other people, including the Montgolfiers, had tried to fill paper or cloth bags with hydrogen, but the gas had leaked out through the walls of the bags. Professor Charles had learned that if silk was coated with a thin layer of rubber, the hydrogen could not escape. When he launched his balloon from Paris a few weeks before the Montgolfiers arrived with theirs, people were so interested that they stayed to watch even after they were soaked by rain. Professor Charles's balloon floated 15 miles into the countryside, landing near a small

village. The villagers, who thought the balloon was a monster, destroyed it with their pitchforks.

The first person ever to go up in a balloon was a young scientist named Jean François Pilâtre de Rozier. His balloon was built by the Montgolfiers and it was attached to the ground by a long rope so that it could not fly away. Then, on November 21, 1783, Pilâtre de Rozier and a nobleman, the Marquis d'Arlandes, became the first people to ride in a balloon that flew freely through the air. This balloon carried a heat source. The two men fed straw and wool into the fire when they wanted the balloon to go higher and let the fire die down when they wanted the balloon to sink. They spent part of their historic flight putting out small fires that had spread to the ropes and envelope (cloth covering) of their balloon. Still, they were able to stay aloft for 25 minutes and land safely. The French crowds watched with wonder—and so did Benjamin Franklin, who was then the United States ambassador to France.

BY ABOUT 1800, people realized that hydrogen balloons were easier to fly than hot-air balloons. A hot-air balloon needed to carry a fire as a source of heat. Having that fire spread was always a danger, as Pilâtre de Rozier and the marquis had discovered. But hydrogen would keep a balloon in the air for as long as the passengers wanted. When the balloonists decided to land, they opened a valve and let the gas

A hydrogen balloon, with useless oars, crosses the English Channel, 1785.

out little by little until the balloon sank to the ground. Also, hydrogen is much lighter than hot air, so a hydrogen-filled balloon is able to lift a greater weight than a hot-air balloon of the same size.

Unfortunately, hydrogen balloons were also dangerous. Hydrogen gas burns so easily that a single spark could set fire to a balloon and destroy it in seconds. Even a spark of static electricity caused by the tearing of the envelope could create an explosion. Still, in spite of the dangers, riding in balloons or watching other people ride in them were popular entertainments during the 1800s.

All the early balloons shared another problem: A free-floating balloon can go only where the wind takes it. Early balloonists could control how high they rose, but not the direction in which they flew. To be useful as transportation, a balloon would have to have a power source and be able to be steered—it had to be *dirigible*. During the 1800s, many people tried to invent dirigible balloons. Their less successful designs used oars, giant sails, and harnessed eagles.

In 1852, the French engineer Henri Giffard hung a gondola (the car in which passengers ride) beneath a cigar-shaped hydrogen balloon. The gondola had a steam engine and a propeller; the balloon had a canvas rudder that could be moved from side to side with ropes. This was the first true dirigible, but the motors available at the time were heavy and not very powerful. Giffard's dirigible could travel only 6 miles per hour, so in a wind blowing more than 6 miles per hour, Giffard had no more control over his dirigible than he would have had over a balloon. Only at the very end of the 1800s was a light, powerful engine developed. This engine, fueled by gasoline, was used for dirigibles and also for two new kinds of transportation: automobiles and airplanes.

On October 19, 1901, a small hydrogen-filled dirigible with a gasoline engine was flown from a field outside Paris, around the Eiffel Tower, and then back to its starting point. This seven-mile trip won the pilot, Alberto Santos-Dumont, a prize of 125,000 francs (about $20,000). Santos-Dumont was a wealthy young Brazilian. He had come to Paris dreaming about dirigibles, but when he arrived he discovered that none had been flown there for almost 15 years. Surprised and disappointed, he began to design balloons. Then he designed and piloted his first dirigible. He was flying his sixth when he won his prize.

Santos-Dumont could often be seen sailing above the rooftops of Paris in his dirigible *Number 9*. He liked to park it outside his favorite café. While he drank his coffee or wine, the 36-foot-long dirigible blocked the street and tied up traffic.

But Santos-Dumont's dirigibles were never a practical way for one or two people to travel. Soon after the Wright brothers made their first airplane flight in 1903, a faster and less expensive way to fly became available. Even Santos-Dumont abandoned dirigibles for

FOLLOWING PAGES: *Santos-Dumont flies his dirigible around the Eiffel Tower.*

planes. In 1906 he made the first airplane flight in Europe, piloting a plane he had helped to design. Later, when airplanes and dirigibles were used in wars, he was sorry that he had helped develop them.

INVENTORS HOPED THAT lighter-than-air craft would be able to do something early planes could not: carry large numbers of passengers or heavy cargo. An airplane is heavier than air, so it needs most of its engines' power just to stay aloft. A dirigible was lighter than air, but to carry more weight, it had to be bigger—which created problems. A larger dirigible needed greater power in order to move through the air and a support system to keep the envelope from bending and twisting in the wind.

Many people tried to solve these problems, but the best solutions came from one man: Count Ferdinand von Zeppelin of Germany. In 1900, when von Zeppelin launched his first dirigible, he was already 61 years old. He had been an army officer, and it was only after his retirement that he began to design dirigibles, but he had been thinking about them for many years. In the 1860s, during the American Civil War, von Zeppelin had been impressed by the Union Army's use of balloons. Observers in tethered balloons had been able to telegraph news of battles to people on the ground and to make maps showing the location of enemy camps. Von Zeppelin believed that dirigibles could become important military weapons.

Count von Zeppelin and his airship no. 11, The Viktoria Luise

Count von Zeppelin's first dirigible was the result of many years of study and experimentation. It was about 420 feet long. Inside was a stiff frame made of aluminum—a strong, lightweight metal that had just been discovered. A long row of gasbags, which would contain hydrogen, was placed inside the frame. The whole structure was covered with tightly stretched cloth.

For greater power, the count used several gasoline engines, which turned large propellers. Elevator flaps (to help raise or lower the craft) and rudders were controlled by a system of cables and pulleys. Von Zeppelin's aircraft was the first that required a crew and a captain, as a ship does. Although dirigibles of that type are called rigid airships because of their stiff framework, they are also called zeppelins in honor of the man who invented them.

The count continued to experiment. When his dirigibles crashed, he learned from his mistakes. By 1910, he had a fleet of reliable zeppelins that carried mail and passengers among German cities. It was the world's first airline, and for the four years of its existence it flew without a single accident.

After World War I began in August 1914, zeppelins began to be used in a new way: The German army sent them on raids. This was the first time airships had carried weapons. Von Zeppelin had been right about the airship's usefulness in war. Zeppelins could fly hundreds of miles without refueling. Under cover of darkness, they crossed the North Sea to drop bombs on England. English people listened for the drone of the engines and the whistle of the falling bombs, then waited in fear for the explosions. In 1914, wars were still fought mostly by soldiers on foot and on horseback. Zeppelins changed the way wars were fought—and their use in war changed the way people looked at zeppelins. Airships came to be seen as evil and terrible.

At first the zeppelin raids were usually successful, but as World War I continued, the Allied Forces (England, the United States, and the other countries that fought on their side) were able to shoot down the airships. Guns shot at them from the ground. Later in the war, airplanes carried guns into the air. The small planes were flimsy, but fast and agile; and the huge, slow zeppelins filled with explosive hydrogen were easy targets. Of all the zeppelins sent out on raids, about half were shot down.

During World War I, the Allies also used dirigibles—not the large, rigid zeppelins, but smaller, flexible craft called blimps. These blimps were used as escorts for fleets of ships. An observer in the blimp could get a glimpse of enemy submarines before they could attack the ships.

DURING THE WAR, German airship technology was greatly improved. The last of the World War I zeppelins were nearly 700 feet long and

FOLLOWING PAGES: *German airships are caught in searchlights over England in WWI.*

could travel 60 miles per hour. But in 1918, when the Germans lost the war, they were forbidden to make airships. For many years the great Zeppelin Company manufactured only aluminum pots and pans. In the years after World War I, several other countries built airships—for exploration, for military purposes, and to carry goods and passengers.

Airships had been used for exploration even before the war. In 1906, an American named Walter Wellman had tried to fly a dirigible to the North Pole but had failed. Then in 1907, he tried to fly across the Atlantic Ocean. He, his five crew members, and a stowaway cat were all rescued after the engines stopped working, but Wellman gave up flying.

By the 1920s, polar exploration still excited many people and airships were more reliable. In 1925, the Norwegian explorer Roald Amundsen tried to fly to the North Pole by airplane but had to give up when his plane was damaged. Amundsen's next try was made in a small airship, the *Norge*. It was piloted by its Italian designer, Umberto Nobile, and paid for by an American. This time the flight was a success. On May 12, 1926, the crew of the *Norge* dropped Norwegian, Italian, and American flags at the North Pole, then continued across the Arctic to Alaska. Amundsen had achieved his goal—one week after Richard E. Byrd had succeeded in flying to the North Pole in an airplane.

The Norge *leaves its hangar in Norway for the flight over the North Pole.*

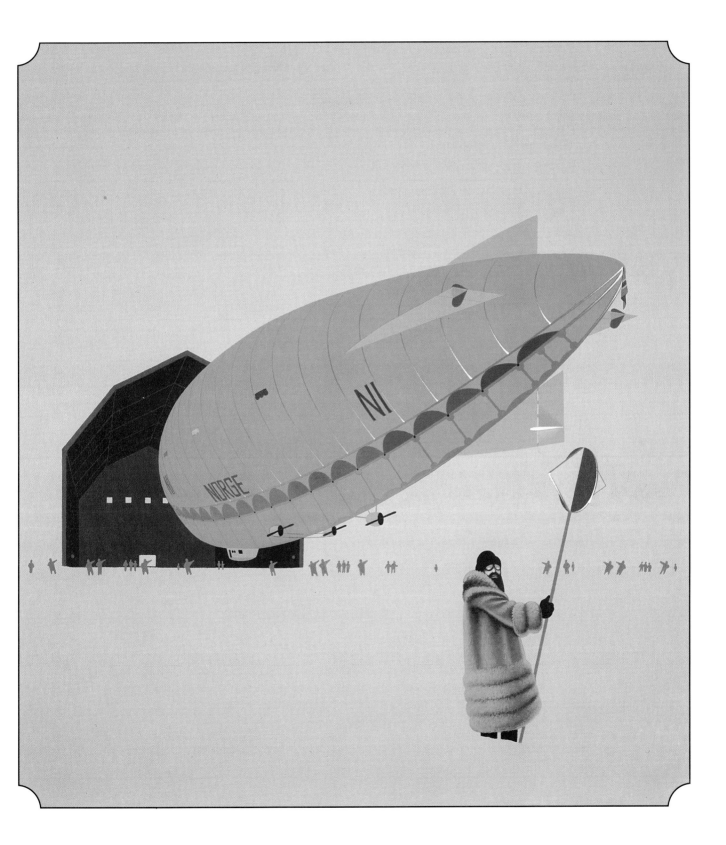

After the expedition, Nobile and Amundsen argued about who deserved more credit for their successful flight. Amundsen even complained that Nobile had dropped too many Italian flags out the window! Annoyed at Amundsen and fascinated by his glimpse of the Arctic, Nobile decided to return with a different airship and crew. He and a ship called the *Italia* were able to reach the North Pole, but there they were caught in a storm. Ice formed on the airship, weighing it down. As it crashed, many of the crew, Nobile's dog, and several crates of supplies were thrown onto the ice. Suddenly lighter, the *Italia* shot up into the fog and disappeared, with six men still on board.

After surviving on the ice for many weeks, eating the supplies that had fallen out of the airship (and the meat of a polar bear that someone shot), a few of the crew members were rescued. Others died—as did Roald Amundsen, whose airplane disappeared somewhere in the Arctic while he was searching for the *Italia*'s survivors.

AFTER THE WAR, a few passenger airships were built in England. In 1919, one of them—the R-34—flew from England to New York and back, the first aircraft of any kind to make a round trip across the Atlantic Ocean. After this success, the English held a competition between two teams of designers and engineers, one from a private company, the other from the government. Each would build a huge passenger airship. The group that constructed the better aircraft would be awarded a government contract to build several more.

After working for about five years, both teams finished their ships at almost the same time. The R-100, built by the private company, was a well-designed airship; but the government's R-101 had a number of serious flaws. Among other problems, it was too heavy and its elevator flaps worked poorly. Some of the problems were quickly repaired and—without proper testing and with the last-minute installation of several tons of carpeting—the R-101 left for India.

Night fell as the doomed airship crossed the English Channel. High winds tossed the ship around and the gasbags inside began to leak, causing the ship to lose altitude. By the time the R-101 reached France, it was flying so low that French farmers were awakened by the noise of its engines as it passed. Then it crashed into the ground and exploded. Forty-eight people died, and the British public was so outraged that the country's airship program was ended. The R-100 was sold as scrap.

During the same period of time, the Americans designed the *Akron* and the *Macon,* which were flying aircraft carriers. Each airship was about 785 feet long and held 5 small airplanes inside its hull, beneath the gasbags. A plane could be lowered into the air on a hook, fly a mission, and return to the zeppelin. This system combined the advantages of both craft: An airship could fly longer distances; an airplane was faster and could change direction more easily.

The most important contribution the United States made to airship technology was the discovery that gasbags could be filled with helium gas. Helium is almost as light as hydrogen and does not burn, so it is much safer. But the only source of helium was a mine in Kansas, which made helium expensive and scarce. It was used only in American airships.

In 1925, the ban on German airship construction was ended, and the Zeppelin Company began work on a new passenger airship. Count von Zeppelin had died in 1917, but his company continued under the leadership of Dr. Hugo Eckener, who was an experienced and talented pilot. The new airship was ready in 1928. Called the *Graf Zeppelin* (*Graf* is German for "Count"), it was 775 feet long, needed 40 crew members, and had space for 20 passengers.

From the beginning, the *Graf Zeppelin* was a success. It made flights between Germany and the United States, as well as around Europe. In 1929, the airship made history by flying around the world in less than 22 days. Having shown that the airship was fast and safe, Eckener piloted regularly scheduled passenger flights between Europe and South America. Not since Count von Zeppelin's prewar airline had there been an air service so reliable—and never had there been one so elegant.

A voyage on the *Graf Zeppelin* was glamorous, comfortable, and expensive. Although it cost about the same as a first-class ticket on an ocean liner, it was much faster. And travel by air was still new to most people. It was an adventure. The passenger area in the rear of the gondola included staterooms and a combination lounge/dining room, all with lightweight aluminum, wicker, and cloth furniture.

During its 9 years of service, the *Graf Zeppelin* made 590 flights—totaling more than 1,000,000 miles—without an accident. Good engineering and design played a part in its success. So did the personality of Hugo Eckener. His experience as a pilot helped him to judge what the airship could do safely, and no one could ever convince him to do something he believed was unsafe. The *Graf Zeppelin,* nicknamed "The Queen of the Skies," was the most graceful, reliable, and beautiful airship ever built.

In the early years of the *Graf Zeppelin*'s success, the future of airship travel seemed secure. The great airships of the 1920s and '30s were magnificent machines. They were as long as an ocean liner or an 80-story skyscraper lying on its side. Covered with silvery fabric that shone in the sun, a great airship sailing serenely overhead was a majestic sight. Airplanes were becoming faster and safer, but airships provided a different experience of flight. The passenger area was far away from the engines, so flight was almost silent. Even at top speed—85 miles per hour—an airship seemed to be in slow motion.

FOLLOWING PAGES: *The* Graf Zeppelin *flies over the pyramids in Egypt.*

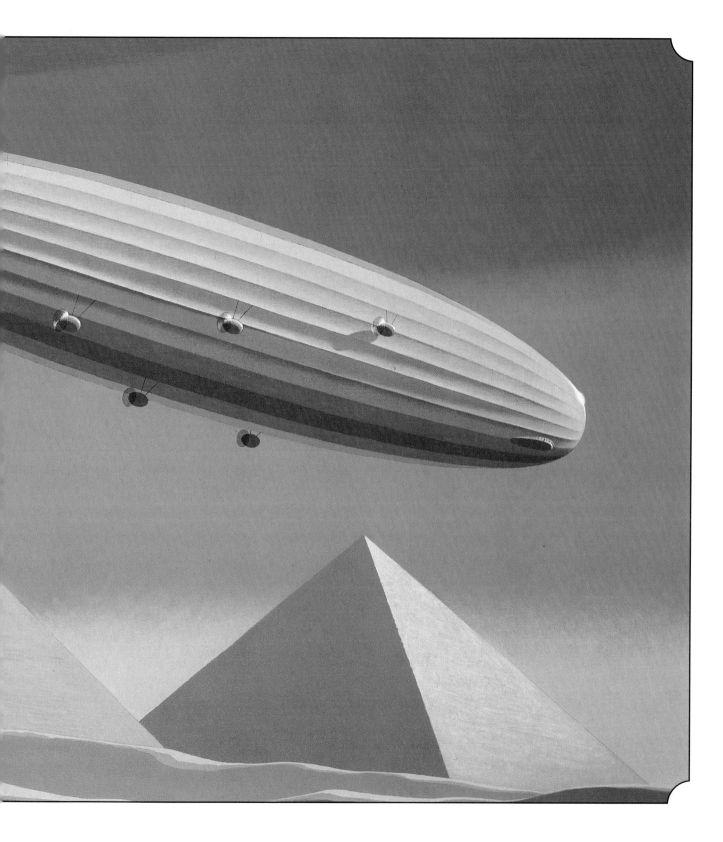

Passengers, free to move around, watched the earth passing below them from a peaceful platform in the sky. During World War I, zeppelins had been frightening, but now their sleek, streamlined shape became a symbol of the Modern Age.

In 1936, the Zeppelin Company launched a new airship: the *Hindenburg*. It was the world's largest and most luxurious zeppelin. Over 800 feet long, it had room for 50 passengers on two levels. It had lounges, cabins, dining rooms, and decks with picture windows. It even had an aluminum piano. The *Hindenburg*'s designers had hoped to fill it with helium, but the United States still controlled the world's supply. The American government had begun to have political disagreements with Germany's new Nazi government and refused to sell any helium to the German company. The ship was filled with hydrogen instead.

The *Hindenburg* made 56 flights safely. Then, on May 6, 1937, the ship flew to the United States from Germany. New Yorkers looked up to see the airship floating over the skyscrapers, the swastikas on its tail fins clearly visible. A few hours later, while the *Hindenburg* was docking at Lakehurst, New Jersey, there was a small flash of light at one end of the airship. Thirty-two seconds later it had been destroyed by explosions and lay in flames on the ground. Of the 97 people on board, a surprising number walked or jumped from the burning ship and survived, but 36 died. No one has ever determined

The explosion of the Hindenburg

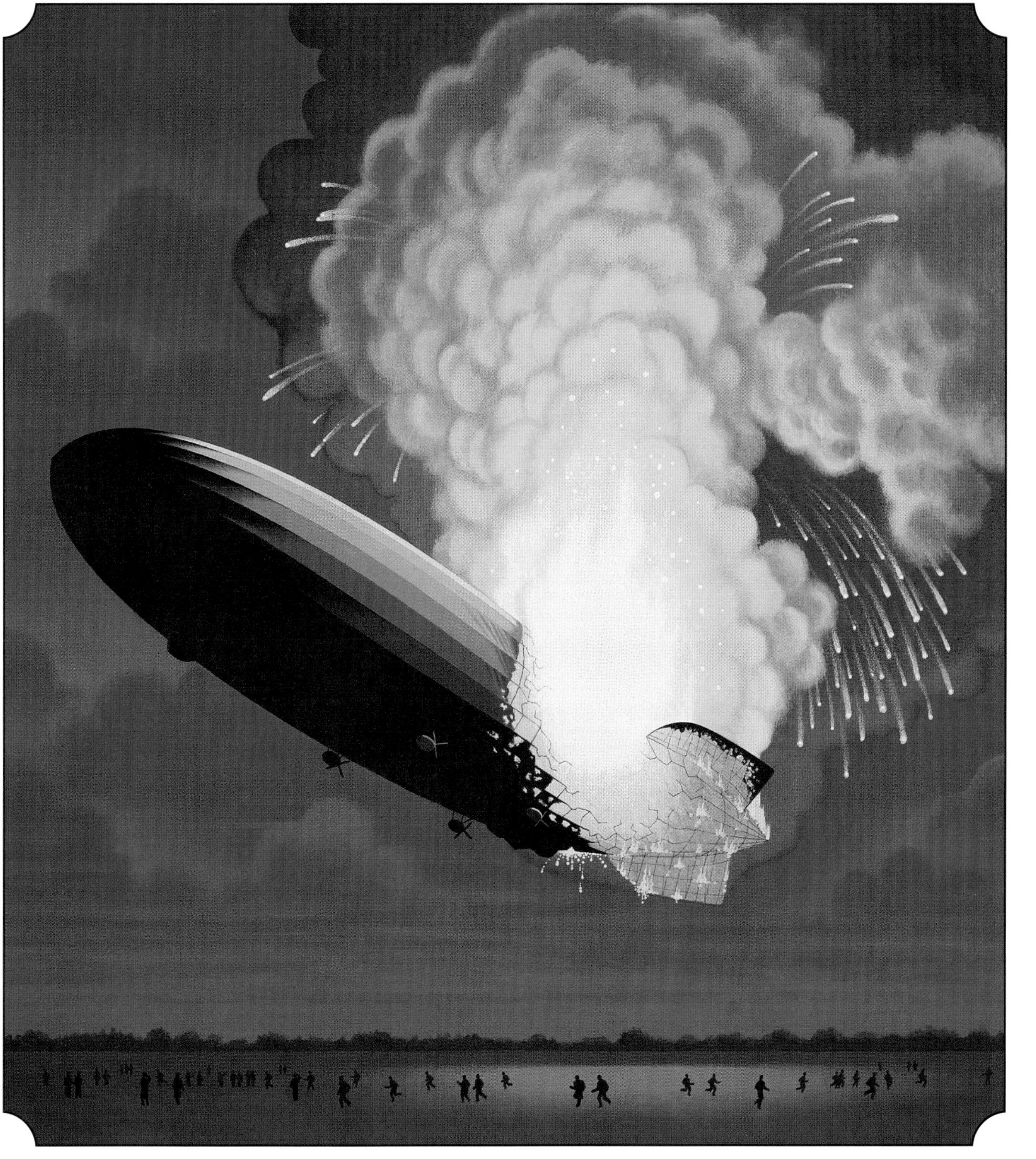

what caused the explosion. Lightning, static electricity, human error, and sabotage against the Nazis have all been suggested.

There had been too many airship disasters. Despite the safety of helium, the *Akron* had crashed in 1933 in a thunderstorm. Two years later the *Macon* had been wrecked when high winds ripped away one of its fins. The *Hindenburg* was the last of the great airships. Its explosion was broadcast live over the radio, and films of the disaster were shown in movie theater newsreels. Giant airships were never built after that. Airplanes were now able to fly long distances carrying many passengers and heavy cargo. When World War II began, planes—not zeppelins—were the most important air weapons.

THE STORY OF lighter-than-air travel is mainly the story of failures. People who designed airships made many mistakes—often because they were experimenting with new technology, sometimes because they were careless. But even the best-designed airships were made of an easily broken metal framework covered with fabric, and carried heavy engines. Airships filled with hydrogen could explode. All airships could be damaged by bad weather. Rain or ice weighed them down; strong winds made them impossible to steer or land safely. Yet for years airships continued to be built by people fascinated with the challenge of solving those technical problems—and, sometimes, by people interested in making money or winning wars.

Today, blimps one quarter the length of the *Hindenburg* are used as flying billboards and to hold cameras for sports events. Balloons are still used for scientific research and for weather forecasting. And recently some scientists and members of the armed forces have argued that, with the help of modern technology, airships could safely be used for lifting heavy machinery. The story of lighter-than-air travel may not be over.

Beginning in the 1960s, a rebirth of interest in the hot-air balloon brought lighter-than-air travel back to its very beginnings. The Montgolfiers might wonder at modern, tough lightweight fabrics. Propane burners make controlling the air temperature inside balloons much easier than it was when early passengers fed smoky fires with wool and straw. But the new balloons are much like the ones the French brothers invented over 200 years ago. People gather in fields on calm, clear mornings to fill their brightly colored balloons. Rising silently above the earth, drifting with the breeze, passengers can once again enjoy the feeling of flight in a craft that is lighter than air.

FOLLOWING PAGE: *A modern hot-air balloon rally*